Contributors

Alain Rolland
Alnoor Fadhl Alnoor
Angie Hawkins
Bob Crites
Carolyn Watson Dubisch & Mike Dubisch
Dan Ehl
Fil A. Chavez
Christine Maudy
Kevin E. Buckley
Robert A. Walker
Seyed Mosayeb Alam
Sharon Curcio
Bob Brill
Diann Floyd Boehm
Doug Lawrence
Fern Brady
Jackiem Joyner
John Mahaffey
Kristina Rienzi
Peter Pontsa

Review Tales
A Book Magazine For Indie Authors

Founder & Editor in Chief: S. Jeyran Main
Publisher: Review Tales Publishing & Editing Services
Print & Distribution: Ingram Spark
Designs: Pexels
ISBN 978-1-988680-64-4 (Paperback)
ISBN 978-1-988680-65-1 (Digital)
www.jeyranmain.com
For all inquiries, please contact us directly.

Photo Credits from Pexels:
mohamed-weaam-101155890-28055748
cottonbro-7225786
nati-87264186-20522243

Editor's Note

As the world awakens from its winter slumber, we are thrilled to present the fourth edition of Review Tales, marking our inaugural spring issue. This season symbolizes renewal and growth, mirroring our magazine's journey and the literary blossoms we are eager to share with you.

In this edition, we proudly feature 20 meticulously selected book reviews, chosen from an extensive pool of submissions. Each work offers a unique narrative, inviting readers to explore diverse worlds and perspectives. Our selection process was both rigorous and rewarding, aiming to present you with stories that resonate and inspire.

We extend our deepest gratitude to the authors and publishers who have entrusted us with their creations. Your contributions are the lifeblood of our publication, and we are honored to showcase your talents. Your unwavering dedication to the craft of storytelling enriches our literary community and provides our readers with endless avenues of exploration.

To our steadfast supporters—readers, reviewers, and literary enthusiasts—thank you for your continued encouragement. Your passion fuels our mission to celebrate and promote literature. We are immensely grateful for your engagement and the vibrant discussions that stem from our shared love of books.

Spring is a time of transformation and possibility. As nature rejuvenates, we too embrace this season with a renewed commitment to bringing you insightful and engaging content. We hope this issue not only introduces you to compelling reads but also inspires personal growth and reflection.

In the spirit of spring, we encourage you to immerse yourself in the stories within these pages. Let them be a source of inspiration and a reminder of the beauty that literature brings to our lives.

Editor-in-Chief
Review Tales Magazine

SPRING 2025 | ISSUE 04

BOOK REVIEWS

Review Tales is thrilled to have reached the milestone of over 1,900 book reviews. With this extensive experience, we've had the privilege of exploring a vast range of literature. Our reviews are always impartial and thoughtfully crafted to highlight authors' strengths while inspiring them to keep creating. For this Spring issue, we've handpicked 20 exceptional book reviews to feature.

TO APPLY FOR A BOOK REVIEW VISIT
WWW.JEYRANMAIN.COM

Book Reviews

SIX YEARS OF ABSENCE BY ALAIN ROLLAND

SHE, ET AL. BY ALNOOR FADHL ALNOOR

RUNNING IN SLIPPERS BY ANGIE HAWKINS

NO GHOSTS IN THE GRAVEYARD BY BOB CRITES

THE PEOPLE THAT MELT IN THE RAIN BY CAROLYN WATSON DUBISCH & MIKE DUBISCH

JAK BARLEY, PRIVATE INQUISITOR AND THE CASE OF THE VERY ANNOYED VIPER MAGES BY DAN EHL

UNUSED TOWELS, FIL CHAVEZ BY FIL A. CHAVEZ

NEVER ALONE BY CHRISTINE MAUDY

THE SECRET SIGN OF THE LIZARD PEOPLE BY KEVIN E. BUCKLEY

TWO CROWNS, THREE BLADES BY ROBERT A. WALKER

VIVID VISIONS BY SEYED MOSAYEB ALAM

ASAYI AN AUTISTIC TEEN'S JOURNEY TO TOPPLE A SHOGUN IN MEDIEVAL JAPAN BY SHARON CURCIO

:5 - SECONDS TO DIE BY BOB BRILL

BOOMER SEE THE TOWN BY DIANN FLOYD BOEHM

GRIEF THE SILENT PANDEMIC BY DOUG LAWRENCE

LOVE'S CALL BY FERN BRADY

MINOR ASSASSIN BY JACKIEM JOYNER

SHAFTED BY JOHN MAHAFFEY

AMONG US BY KRISTINA RIENZI

SANCTITY OF FREEDOM BY PETER PONTSA

THE CAPTIVATING ODYSSEY OF A FRENCH SOLDIER IN WWII
Alain Rolland

Reviewer: Jeyran Main

Six Years of Absence by Alain Rolland offers a gripping account of a French soldier's journey through the horrors of war, imprisonment, and survival. Based on true events, it follows Alexandre, a young soldier whose peaceful life with his wife and newborn child in Brittany is shattered when war is declared in 1939. Enlisted to fight on the Eastern Front, his journey leads him from Flanders to Dunkirk, where he misses the last boat to England and is eventually captured.

Alexandre is marched to Holland and then transported to two prison camps in Pomerania. His five-year confinement at the village of Schivelbein, where he works in a kommando, starts a grueling survival story. Amidst the brutality of war, Alexandre's experiences are tempered with moments of humor and camaraderie, creating a deep emotional connection between the reader and his journey.

Rolland's narrative expertly balances tragedy with moments of lightness, allowing readers to witness the resilience of the human spirit even in the darkest times. Alexandre encounters many endearing characters who bring hope and human connection to his otherwise grim existence. These relationships help him persevere through the torment, offering brief yet precious moments of relief. The pacing of Six Years of Absence is steady and compelling, with each chapter adding tension and suspense. Alexandre's eventual liberation by the Red Army marks a dramatic turning point, but his return to a family he hardly recognizes brings challenges. The changes wrought by six years of absence are profound, making his journey back to normalcy both problematic and emotionally complex.

Rolland's honesty about the brutality of war, combined with heartbreaking twists and turns, makes this novel a must-read for fans of historical fiction. Six Years of Absence is an unforgettable story of survival, love, and the unbreakable human spirit. It reminds readers that even in the darkest of times, there is hope and, through endurance, the strength to reclaim life.

SHE, ET AL.
Alnoor Fadhl Alnoor

Reviewer: Jeyran Main

She, et al. by Alnoor Fadhl Alnoor is a groundbreaking work of fiction that shatters conventional storytelling to present a gripping and thought-provoking exploration of courage, resilience, and the human spirit. Through the eyes of its compelling heroines, the novel delves into the harrowing scars of war, the weight of societal taboos, and the relentless pursuit of justice against a backdrop of corruption.

From the very first page, Alnoor draws the reader into a world where survival is an act of defiance. The narrators—each a unique voice, yet part of a collective journey—share their experiences with raw honesty and vulnerability. Their words are often whispered in quiet moments of reflection, but just as often, they explode onto the page with unflinching truths that demand to be heard. The sharp wit embedded in their narratives adds a layer of complexity, turning what could be a bleak tale of tragedy into one of surprising empowerment.

The weight of war hangs heavy over She, et al., but it's not merely a story of violence. Alnoor takes readers deep into the emotional landscape of these heroines, showing how the scars left by conflict shape their identities and their quest for justice. What makes this novel especially captivating is its exploration of societal taboos and how those who live under the constraints of these unspoken rules struggle to break free in search of their own truth.

In addition to the intimate, personal accounts, the novel tackles broader themes of corruption and societal injustice, using the characters' journeys as a mirror for the world around us. The struggle for justice, as portrayed in the book, is not just about the legal system—it's about confronting the systems that oppress and silence.

Alnoor's poetic and powerful writing captures the tension between despair and hope. The heroines' journeys are fraught with peril, but their struggles reveal the narrative's valid message: in the face of adversity, there is always a flicker of hope, and with hope, there is the potential for triumph.

She, et al. is a novel that will resonate long after turning the final page. It challenges readers to reconsider their convictions, confront uncomfortable truths, and recognize the strength that lies in vulnerability. This unforgettable story of survival and strength is one that you'll want to experience.

RUNNING IN SLIPPERS
Angie Hawkins

Reviewer: Jeyran Main

In Running in Slippers, Angie Hawkins opens her heart and mind in a raw, witty memoir about the personal crisis that turned her life upside down. Written with humor and brutal honesty, Hawkins takes readers on a journey through her grief after a failed relationship and the loss of her father. The result is a profoundly vulnerable narrative that feels like an emotional rollercoaster from which you can't look away.

Hawkins begins with the relatable notion of using distractions to fill the void left by trauma. However, her misguided attempts at escapism—from poorly planned decisions to desperate fixes—are exposed with self-awareness and wit. This is not a polished, perfect account of overcoming adversity. Instead, it's a messy, unfiltered glimpse into the human experience, especially when we feel most broken.

The memoir's strength lies in Hawkins' refusal to hide her imperfections. In a world dominated by social masks and digital facades, she challenges the notion that vulnerability is something to fear. Rather than offering an idealized version of herself, she embraces the awkward, painful, and often funny moments that many of us try to keep hidden. This authenticity invites readers to connect, reminding us that we don't need to be perfect to be worthy of belonging.

Hawkins' sharp wit provides much-needed levity as she explores the darker parts of her journey. Her writing has an almost confessional tone that allows the reader to feel as though they're sitting across from her, sharing in her mistakes and triumphs. The impact of the COVID-19 pandemic on society and the disconnection many people felt during this time add an extra layer to her message. Running in Slippers calls for more honest, genuine connections in a world increasingly dominated by curated online personas.

At times, the book's rawness may be unsettling for some, but that's also what makes it so powerful. Hawkins' story is one of resilience, not through perfection but through embracing the messiness of life. This memoir proves that even in our most vulnerable moments, we can find the courage to be accurate. If you're looking for a book as funny as it is heart-wrenching, Running in Slippers is one you won't want to miss.

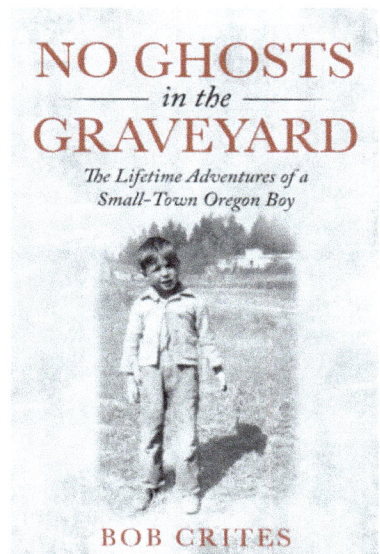

NO GHOSTS IN THE GRAVEYARD
Bob Crites

Reviewer: Jeyran Main

No Ghosts in the Graveyard: The Life-Time Adventures of a Small-Town Oregon Boy by Bob Crites is a heartwarming and adventurous memoir that takes readers on a journey through the author's early life. The book is filled with humor, challenges, and unexpected moments of growth. Crites' personal story resonates with those who appreciate tales of resilience, personal development, and the determination to make a difference in the world. His narrative is captivating and relatable, providing a glimpse into a life well-lived.

In this memoir, Crites reflects on his childhood in Eugene, Oregon, where he spent his days selling newspapers as a nine-year-old, one of the last American paperboys. Living in the 1950s, he and his triplet siblings didn't understand the concept of homelessness; to them, their situation felt more like a camping adventure in the woods with their young mother. This early experience shapes Crites' worldview, marking the beginning of a life filled with curiosity, resourcefulness, and a sense of adventure. His perspective on life is optimistic and adaptable, which stays with him throughout the book.

The memoir chronicles Crites' path from a young boy navigating life's difficulties to an adult determined to help others. He finds his true calling in social work, where his passion for helping people shines through. His journey is not without challenges—Crites recounts both the funny and the tragic moments that have shaped him into the person he is today. Whether it's saving lives, risking his own, or making a profound impact on the lives of young people, Crites' story is a testament to perseverance, empathy, and the power of making a difference. His stories, both humorous and poignant, create a deeply engaging narrative.

Crites' writing is engaging, relatable, and filled with a dry wit that adds depth to the narrative. His reflections on life's twists and turns make for a compelling read, with a balance of humor and heartfelt moments that will resonate with readers from all walks of life. His voice is genuine, allowing readers to connect with him.

No Ghosts in the Graveyard celebrates resilience, community, and the power of helping others. Crites' journey from a small-town Oregon boy to a compassionate adult is worth reading, leaving readers with hope and inspiration. This book is a must-read for anyone interested in memoirs that highlight personal growth and one person's impact on the world.

THE PEOPLE THAT MELT IN THE RAIN
Carolyn Watson Dubisch & Mike Dubisch

Reviewer: Jeyran Main

Carolyn Watson-Dubisch's The People That Melt in the Rain, The Traveling Show is an imaginative and eerie tale that weaves mystery, magic, and adventure into a compelling narrative. With striking illustrations by Mike Dubisch, this Kindle edition delivers a captivating experience for readers who enjoy stories filled with supernatural intrigue.

At the heart of the story is 12-year-old Laura, whose life takes a surreal and unsettling turn when she finds herself trapped inside a painting in the school library. But this is no ordinary work of art—it holds the secrets of her new town, Deluge, a place bound by a dark and peculiar curse. As Laura navigates this magical realm, she must unravel the mystery behind the town's tragic fate and discover a way to break the spell that has held its people hostage. The stakes are high, and her freedom hangs in the balance.

Watson-Dubisch crafts a haunting atmosphere, blending elements of fantasy and folklore with a sense of childlike wonder. The premise—being trapped in a painting—evokes a timeless, almost fairy-tale-like quality, reminiscent of classic stories where children stumble upon hidden worlds. Laura's predicament creates immediate tension, drawing readers into her plight and making them eager to uncover the town's buried secrets.

One of the book's most substantial aspects is its ability to immerse readers in a setting that feels whimsical and foreboding. Deluge, as a cursed town, holds an aura of mystery that keeps the reader engaged, and Laura's determination to break free makes her a relatable and compelling protagonist. The presence of magic adds an extra layer of excitement, making the book a fantastic read for middle-grade audiences who enjoy stories with a gothic or supernatural edge.

Mike Dubisch's illustrations enhance the book's eerie yet enchanting quality. His artwork adds depth to the storytelling, helping to bring Laura's strange adventure to life in a way that words alone might not fully capture.

Overall, The People That Melt in the Rain, The Traveling Show is a spellbinding read filled with mystery, adventure, and just the right amount of darkness. It's perfect for young readers who love eerie tales with a dash of magic, making it a worthy addition to any fantasy lover's collection.

JAK BARLEY, PRIVATE INQUISITOR AND THE CASE OF THE VERY ANNOYED VIPER MAGES
Dan Ehl

Reviewer: Jeyran Main

Jak Barley, Private Inquisitor and the Case of the Very Annoyed Viper Mages by Dan Ehl takes readers on another delightful, action-packed journey with Jak Barley, the sharp-witted and ever-curious private inquisitor. Jak hopes for a well-deserved break after successfully solving his previous case involving a covert assassin at the Duburoake Royal Menagerie. However, his plans are quickly upended when a series of attacks disrupt the crystal ball network of the country's witch covens, and a pixie gold shipment mysteriously disappears.

In this latest adventure, Jak is plunged into a web of intrigue, fraught with danger and the looming threat of viper mages—powerful, vengeful magic users who aren't thrilled with Jak's involvement in their affairs. The stakes are high, and Jak's usual mix of wit, resourcefulness, and sheer determination are tested as he untangles a trail of curses, betrayal, and peril.

Jak's adventures wouldn't be complete without his trusty companions. This time, he enlists the help of his enigmatic friend, Lorenzo Spasm, who hails from an alternate universe where magic doesn't exist. Lorenzo's unique ability to turn curses back on their casters creates a fun—and often hilarious—dynamic as the pair faces increasingly dangerous magical forces. Jak's intended, Morgana, a witch-in-training with impressive magical abilities, adds skill and charm to the team, though her powers are still growing and evolving.

While the plot offers an engaging mix of mystery, magic, and humor, there are moments when the pacing slows, and the complexity of the magical elements might overwhelm newcomers to the series. That being said, for fans of the Jak Barley books, this latest installment delivers more of the quirky charm and high-stakes action they've come to love.

Ehl's writing continues to be a delightful blend of fantasy and humor. Sharp dialogue and unexpected twists keep the story captivating. The relationships between Jak, Lorenzo, and Morgana continue to evolve, adding depth and richness to the characters.

Though The Case of the Very Annoyed Viper Mages may not be the most groundbreaking entry in the series, it is a solid and enjoyable addition for fans. It's a clever mix of magic, mystery, and humor that leaves readers eager to see what Jak Barley will tackle next.

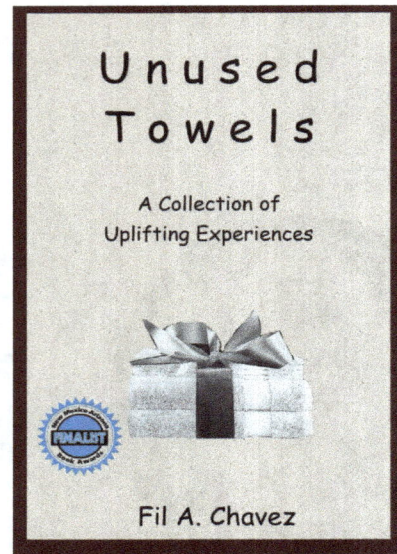

UNUSED TOWELS
Fil A. Chavez

Reviewer: Jeyran Main

Unused Towels by Fil A. Chavez is a powerful and poignant exploration of the misunderstood struggle with suicidal depression. Through a delicate blend of honesty, humor, and raw emotion, Chavez shares his deeply personal journey of battling despair and finding hope through faith. His story speaks directly to those who have wrestled with depression or who seek to understand and support a loved one grappling with suicidal thoughts.

Chavez's approach to the complex subject matter of suicide is courageous and unflinching. He openly recounts his painful experiences, revealing the moments that helped him heal and those that hindered his progress. His narrative is unapologetically raw, offering a rare glimpse into the mind of someone who has been entrenched in the darkness of depression. What makes Unused Towels particularly impactful, however, is the balance Chavez maintains between the heavy emotional weight of his story and the lighter, humorous anecdotes that punctuate the book. These moments of humor offer readers much-needed relief, allowing them to process the more intense sections without diminishing the seriousness of the topic.

The book transcends the author's personal experience, offering valuable insights into the nature of suicide and how others can support those in crisis. Chavez's reflections are beneficial for friends and family of individuals struggling with suicidal thoughts. His practical and compassionate advice on how to reach someone who feels hopeless provides tangible guidance for those who want to intervene but don't know where to start.

Unused Towels has had a profound impact on its readers. One person shared that it helped them better understand their father's struggles with depression before his passing. Another praised the book for providing them with renewed hope after battling their mental health challenges. Even veterans who have experienced war trauma have found solace in Chavez's words, recognizing the book as a source of healing on their journeys.

Ultimately, Unused Towels is a testament to survival, redemption, and hope. It underscores the power of faith, resilience, and love to overcome even the darkest moments. Chavez's willingness to share his vulnerabilities and lessons learned makes this book invaluable for anyone questioning the value of life or how to help others navigate their despair. It reminds us that even in our darkest hours, hope always exists for a brighter tomorrow.

NEVER ALONE: A JOURNEY FROM PAIN TO LOVE
Christine Maudy

Reviewer: Jeyran Main

Never Alone: A Journey From Pain to Love by Christine Maudy is an inspiring and heartfelt memoir that chronicles the author's transformative journey toward healing, empowerment, and spiritual awakening. Through her narrative, Christine invites readers to explore her path of self-discovery, which spans continents and cultures, beginning in France and leading her to a profound understanding of herself and the world around her.

Christine's memoir is a personal account and a universal story of resilience and hope. She opens up about some of the darkest moments of her life that tested her spirit and her belief in a higher power. Despite her pain and struggles, Christine's unwavering faith guided her through, helping her find strength in places she never expected. Her journey is one of exploration, not only of the physical world but also of the mysteries beyond the material realm, as she uncovers truths about life, purpose, and the spiritual forces that shape our paths. Each chapter offers a deeper look into how Christine's connection to the divine significantly affected her healing.

Throughout the book, Christine shares valuable lessons learned along the way—lessons that remind readers of their own inner power and the importance of listening to the guidance that's available to us all. Her story encourages self-reflection and the belief that we are never truly alone, no matter our challenges. She emphasizes the importance of trusting in oneself and the divine forces that provide us with direction, love, and support, even in our darkest moments. This is a powerful message for readers looking for strength during difficult times.

Never Alone is a beacon of inspiration, offering a roadmap for anyone seeking to break free from past limitations and live a life of purpose and meaning. Writer and arts advocate Sandra Conte praised it as a "standout read. This memoir resonates deeply with anyone on a journey of self-discovery or looking for inspiration. Christine's journey is a testament to the power of love, faith, and resilience, making Never Alone a powerful read for anyone needing hope and empowerment.

Christine Maudy's work will give readers a renewed sense of purpose and remind them that we are all connected to something greater than ourselves. Whether readers seek inspiration or enjoy a beautifully written memoir, Never Alone will stay with them long after the last page.

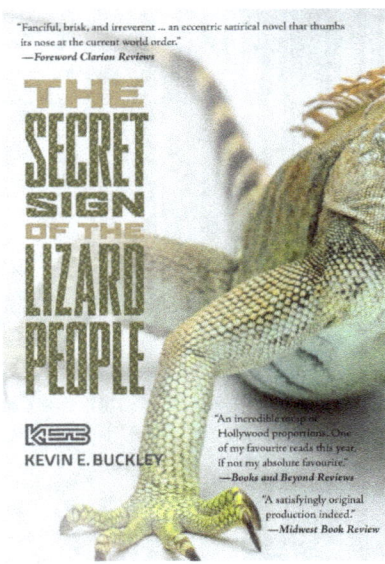

THE SECRET SIGN OF THE LIZARD PEOPLE
Kevin E. Buckley

Reviewer: Jeyran Main

Kevin E. Buckley's The Secret Sign of the Lizard People is a hilarious, fast-paced, and wildly entertaining conspiracy thriller that blends detective noir with sci-fi absurdity. Packed with satire, action, and a cast of eccentric characters, this book offers a tongue-in-cheek take on government cover-ups, global conspiracies, and the ever-popular trope of reptilian overlords secretly ruling the world.

The story follows LAPD homicide detectives Jerry "Leafy" Green and Bill "Beefy" Goodness—two seasoned crime solvers who find themselves entangled in a case far beyond the usual scope of their investigations. When a fashion model is discovered murdered at the Hollywood Sign, it quickly becomes apparent that this is no ordinary homicide. As they dig deeper, Leafy and Beefy uncover a sinister plot that threatens not only Los Angeles but the entire planet.

The plot unfolds in a whirlwind of bizarre twists and escalating stakes as the detectives are forced to assemble a team of unlikely allies to stop an impending global catastrophe. Their crew includes a Jesus-lookalike ufologist, a graffiti artist with street smarts, a top-tier geneticist, a cyber genius, and a fire-and-brimstone reverend—each contributing their unique skills to the mission. The result is a ragtag team that feels like something out of an action-comedy film, filled with witty banter, oddball chemistry, and plenty of laugh-out-loud moments.

Buckley's writing shines in its ability to blend humor with suspense. The sharp and fast-paced dialogue gives the characters distinct personalities that leap off the page. The absurdity of the plot is balanced by strong pacing and clever storytelling, making even the most outlandish elements— like the idea of elite reptilian overlords—feel weirdly plausible within the book's world. The satirical undertones add another layer of depth, poking fun at conspiracy culture, media influence, and government secrecy.

While the novel leans heavily into humor and exaggeration, it still delivers an engaging mystery with thrilling twists. Fans of satirical detective stories, action-packed adventures, and over-the-top sci-fi conspiracies will find plenty to love in The Secret Sign of the Lizard People. It's a wild, unpredictable, and thoroughly enjoyable ride that refuses to take itself too seriously—making it the perfect read for those looking for a fresh and funny take on the crime thriller genre.

TWO CROWNS, THREE BLADES
Robert A. Walker

Reviewer: Jeyran Main

Two Crowns, Three Blades by Robert A. Walker is a thrilling continuation of the Legends of Baelon series. It immerses readers in political intrigue, profound personal loss, and the relentless pursuit of revenge. This action-packed fantasy novel delves into the complex lives of its characters as they navigate their quests for justice and redemption amid the turmoil of war.

The story opens with King Axil of Aranox, still grieving the devastating loss of his wife and daughter, who declares war on the deadly Guild of Takers. His decision to fight against the Guild sets the stage for a brutal conflict, with both sides engaging in a deadly cat-and-mouse game. As the story unfolds, readers are introduced to a cast of compelling characters, each with their motives and allegiances. Tristan Godfrey's search for his brother's murderer intertwines with the larger narrative, while Sibil Dunn embarks on a personal quest for vengeance, determined to right the wrongs that have shaped her life.

One of the standout aspects of Two Crowns, Three Blades is the way Walker weaves together the stories of these characters. While personal motives drive each one, their paths cross in a way that highlights the interconnectedness of their fates. The author expertly balances action and emotional depth, making the stakes feel personal for each character, even as the larger world around them crumbles.

The themes of vengeance and justice run deep throughout the novel, with the characters grappling with the consequences of their actions. As the quest for retribution continues, the book examines the price of revenge and whether it can truly satisfy the wounds of the past.

The world-building in Two Crowns, Three Blades is rich and immersive, with vivid descriptions of the land of Baelon and the political machinations that shape its future. The high stakes of the war, coupled with the characters' struggles, make for a gripping read that keeps you on the edge of your seat.

Fans of epic fantasy with complex characters, intense battles, and a focus on moral dilemmas will find Two Crowns, Three Blades engaging and thought-provoking. Robert A. Walker has crafted a story that explores the cost of revenge and the hope for redemption amidst chaos.

VIVID VISIONS: TALES WOVEN FROM THE THREADS OF DIVERSE IMAGINATIONS
Seyed Mosayeb Alam

Reviewer: Jeyran Main

Vivid Visions is a masterfully crafted collection that will captivate readers from start to finish. Blending elements of horror, romance, suspense, and emotional depth, this anthology is an unforgettable exploration of the human spirit, where love shines brightest in the darkest of moments.

From the first page, Alam's storytelling pulls you into a world of suspense and mystery. The collection is a dynamic blend of chilling terror and heartfelt love, as each story brings characters who are thrust into unimaginable situations to life. Whether facing supernatural horrors or personal demons, these individuals discover that love isn't just an emotion but a powerful force that can guide them through their darkest fears.

The strength of Vivid Visions lies in its ability to evoke emotion. Each narrative delivers a heart-pounding rollercoaster ride filled with unexpected twists, shocking revelations, and moments of profound tenderness. The characters are incredibly relatable, and readers will be emotionally invested in their struggles. As each character faces their nightmare, love emerges as the ultimate weapon in the battle against fear. Whether it's a haunted house or the turmoil of the heart, the book showcases how love can be a beacon of hope, even in the most terrifying circumstances.

The collection also reminds us of the resilience of the human spirit. The journeys in Vivid Visions aren't just about facing external monsters; they also delve into inner fears and the strength it takes to overcome them. With its compelling mix of supernatural thrills and emotional depth, this anthology is a must-read for horror, suspense, and romance fans. Alam's writing is immersive and engaging, creating an atmosphere that pulls you deeper into each story, making it hard to put down.

Whether you're drawn to tales of haunted houses, twisted relationships, or battles against unseen forces, Vivid Visions will keep you hooked. The stories are rich in emotional resonance, reminding us that love can illuminate the way forward, even in fear and darkness.

If you enjoy stories that challenge your perceptions of fear, love, and destiny, Vivid Visions is a must-have for your collection. It will leave you questioning everything you believe about the dark and the light and what it means to conquer your fears truly.

AN AUTISTIC TEEN'S JOURNEY TO TOPPLE A SHOGUN IN MEDIEVAL JAPAN
Sharon Curcio

Reviewer: Jeyran Main

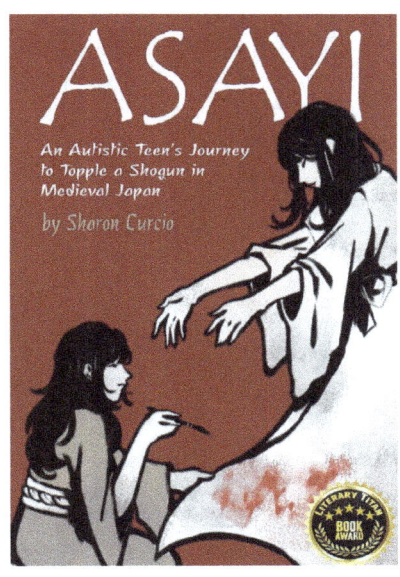

Sharon Curcio's Asayi is a captivating historical novel that masterfully blends political intrigue, social commentary, and an unforgettable protagonist. Set in medieval Japan, it takes readers on an exhilarating journey through a world of deception, power struggles, and resilience in the face of adversity. The story is rich in historical detail, immersing readers in a time when strict social hierarchies dictated one's fate and defying authority came at a steep price.

At the novel's heart is Asayi, an autistic teenager at odds with a brutal regime. Her journey is one of survival, strategy, and self-discovery. Asayi's autism is portrayed with nuance, making her one of historical fiction's most unique and compelling protagonists. She sees the world differently, and in a society that values conformity, her perspective becomes both a liability and a strength. Curcio skillfully illustrates how her sensory experiences, sharp intellect, and keen observation skills set her apart in a world of deception. Readers will find themselves deeply invested in Asayi's growth, as she transforms from a vulnerable girl into a formidable force against oppression.

The novel excels in its world-building, transporting readers to the political turmoil of medieval Japan. The contrast between the rigid court life and the dangerous underworld of society is vividly depicted, adding layers of tension and suspense. From betrayals to unexpected alliances, the novel keeps readers on edge, constantly questioning who can be trusted. The political landscape is not just a backdrop but a living force, shaping characters' destinies and reflecting real-world power struggles.

The supporting cast is equally compelling. From scheming nobles to unexpected allies from society's fringes, every character plays a crucial role in Asayi's fight for justice. Themes of resilience, found family, and social change make Asayi more than just an adventure—it's a powerful reflection on identity and the courage to challenge the status quo.

For fans of historical fiction, political intrigue, and strong character-driven narratives, Asayi is an unforgettable read. With its gripping storytelling and deeply resonant themes, it stands as a testament to the power of perseverance in the face of oppression.

:05 SECONDS TO DIE
Bob Brill

Reviewer: Jeyran Main

:05 Seconds to Die by Bob Brill is a high-octane thriller that combines sharp dialogue, relentless action, and an edge-of-your-seat plot that will leave readers breathless. Set against the backdrop of Los Angeles, with the world's premier sporting event looming, this fast-paced novel introduces P-I Casey Order and his unexpected partner, Ginger Queen, as they race against time to foil a dangerous plot orchestrated by a coalition of ruthless criminal gangs. With their combined skills, a network of allies, and sheer determination, they must stop a massive hack that threatens global economies and the stability of nations.

Brill's writing is cinematic, bringing the reader into the heart of the action. The suspense is palpable, with every twist and turn ratcheting the tension. The novel's film noir influences are evident, particularly in its gritty portrayal of the underworld and its sharp, snappy dialogue that echoes classic detective stories. It's a nod to the golden age of cinema, blending hard-hitting action with a sense of danger and intrigue that never lets up.

Casey Order is at the story's center, a seasoned private investigator whose no-nonsense attitude and relentless drive make him a compelling protagonist. He's joined by Ginger Queen, a sharp and resourceful woman who is the perfect partner in this dangerous mission. The chemistry between the two is palpable, and their dynamic adds a layer of unexpected camaraderie to the otherwise high-stakes narrative—their banter and teamwork help to humanize the characters amid a plot that could change the world forever.

One of the novel's greatest strengths is its pacing. Brill expertly balances heart-pounding action with moments of quiet suspense, keeping readers on the edge. The clock is constantly ticking, and the plot's urgency is felt in every chapter, making it impossible to put the book down.

:5 Seconds to Die is a thrilling international adventure that explores the lengths to which two unlikely heroes will go to protect the world. Its intricate plot, vibrant characters, and relentless pace make it a must-read for fans of action, suspense, and film noir-inspired storytelling. The stakes couldn't be higher, and the payoff is exhilarating.

16

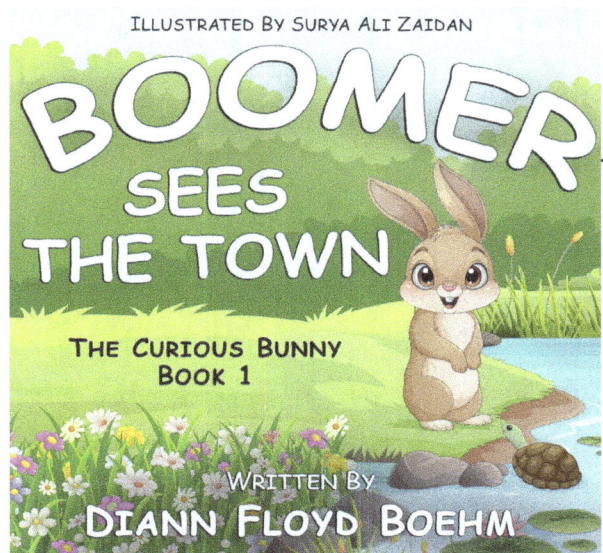

ILLUSTRATED BY SURYA ALI ZAIDAN

BOOMER SEES THE TOWN: THE CURIOUS BUNNY BOOK 1
Diann Floyd Boehm

Reviewer: Jeyran Main

Boomer Sees The Town: The Curious Bunny Book 1 by Diann Floyd Boehm is a delightful and heartwarming tale that transports young readers into the world of Boomer, a curious and adventurous bunny who yearns to explore beyond the comfort of his home. Written for children ages 3 to 9, this charming picture book is perfect for read-aloud sessions with parents and early independent readers alike.

Boomer is not your average bunny. Unlike his brothers and sisters, who are content to stay home, Boomer craves excitement and adventure. He ventures into the city to see what awaits him, encountering a wide range of new characters and experiences. Each page offers a new twist in Boomer's adventure, making this story engaging and full of surprises.

The book's heart lies in portraying Boomer's curiosity and courage. As he enters the unknown, young readers are reminded of the value of exploration, the excitement of discovering new places, and the joy of meeting different others. Through Boomer's experiences, children learn that curiosity and bravery can lead to wonderful things, even if they don't always know what's ahead.

The story is simple yet rich in meaning, making it an ideal choice for parents looking to engage their children in thoughtful conversation. As Boomer interacts with the various characters in the city, he discovers lessons about diversity, kindness, and the importance of trying new things. The pacing is just right for younger readers, with enough detail to keep them intrigued without overwhelming them.

Illustrator Surya Ali Zaidan's vibrant, colorful illustrations bring Boomer's world to life with a playful and inviting style. They add a layer of magic to the story, helping children connect emotionally with the characters and their world.

Boomer Sees The Town is not just an entertaining read but also an educational one. It's an excellent tool for teaching young children about curiosity, courage, and the rewards of stepping outside one's comfort zone. The book's messages of friendship and exploration make it a perfect addition to any child's bookshelf. This is just the first of many adventures for Boomer, and it's easy to see why this lovable bunny will become a favorite character for young readers.

17

GRIEF: THE SILENT PANDEMIC
Doug Lawrence

Reviewer: Jeyran Main

Grief: The Silent Pandemic by Doug Lawrence is an insightful and compassionate exploration of grief, a deeply personal experience often misunderstood and neglected by society. Lawrence, drawing from his extensive experience as a grief mentor and the personal anguish of losing his beloved wife, offers a beacon of hope and understanding for those who are navigating the challenging and often isolating journey of grief.

The book explores grief's emotional, psychological, and societal aspects, shedding light on many individuals' complexities when dealing with loss. Lawrence does an excellent job of addressing the stigma and misconceptions surrounding grief, which often leave people feeling alienated and unsupported. His raw honesty and deep empathy shine through in every chapter, making the book not just a guide but a comforting companion for those in mourning.

Lawrence's ability to blend heartfelt storytelling with practical advice makes Grief: The Silent Pandemic stand out. He provides actionable solutions and tools for healing, giving readers the knowledge and encouragement they need to move forward in their grief journey. His approach is compassionate and empowering, encouraging individuals to embrace their grief, process it, and ultimately heal. The book emphasizes the importance of connection, understanding, and community, urging readers to seek support and share their pain with others who understand.

Lawrence's experience with grief lends the book a sense of authenticity and relatability. His vulnerability and willingness to share his story make the book even more powerful. It's not just a theoretical exploration of grief but a genuine, lived experience that many readers will find comforting. The message is clear: healing is possible, and although grief can feel overwhelming, brighter days lie ahead.

This book is invaluable for anyone experiencing loss or those looking to support a grieving loved one. With its thoughtful, compassionate approach, Grief: The Silent Pandemic offers a much-needed roadmap to healing, breaking the silence around grief, and offering hope to those who need it most.

In a world where grief is often a silent and unspoken burden, Doug Lawrence provides the tools, the understanding, and the compassion necessary to navigate the storm. This book is a powerful reminder that while grief may be silent, we are never truly alone.

LOVE'S CALL
Fern Brady

Reviewer: Jeyran Main

Love's Call by Fern Brady is an enthralling romance that expertly combines political intrigue, a touch of fantasy, and a passionate love story. Set in a world where nations clash, and power dynamics are ever-shifting, the book follows the story of Denipia Leron, a gifted painter, and visionary from Usmerim, who is thrust into an unexpected and complicated relationship with the powerful President Nichamir Linput of Sorusvia.

Denipia, having just won the Innovation Award in the Arts, is thrust into the limelight and soon learns that President Nichamir is not only her patron but has taken a personal interest in her. Initially, Denipia is wary, fearing that this could jeopardize both her burgeoning career and her safety. Her instinct is to keep the charismatic but dangerous leader at arm's length. Yet, she cannot ignore the undeniable attraction she feels toward him.

Nichamir, for his part, is a man of conviction. Having saved his nation from invasion, he has worked tirelessly to ensure prosperity for his people despite the negative propaganda surrounding him. Beneath his robust exterior, however, lies a secret—Nichamir is Dragonborn, a part of him he has kept hidden from the world. From the first moment he meets Denipia, he knows she is his fated mate, and the bond between them is immediate, intense, and impossible to ignore.

The chemistry between the two leads is electric, tension building as Denipia grapples with her feelings for a man she should despise. Brady masterfully captures Denipia's internal conflict—her desire for Nichamir is at odds with her distrust of his political motives and power. At the same time, Nichamir's deep longing to win her trust and prove himself worthy of her love makes for an emotionally charged romance that keeps readers hooked.

Love's Call is more than just a romance; it's a story about trust, power, and destiny. Brady has created a complex world filled with intriguing characters and rich backstories. The dragonborn element adds an exciting fantasy twist to the narrative, giving it a unique flavor that will appeal to readers who enjoy fantasy romance. The stakes are high, and the obstacles in Denipia and Nichamir's relationship are daunting. But through it all, the pull between them is undeniable, and Love's Call leaves readers eagerly anticipating the next chapter in their journey.

This is a captivating and heartwarming read that will resonate with fans of romantic fantasy and political intrigue. Love's Call is a beautiful exploration of love's transformative power, and Fern Brady delivers an unforgettable story that will stay with readers long after the final page.

MINOR ASSASSIN
Jackiem Joyner

Reviewer: Jeyran Main

Minor Assassin by Jackiem Joyner is a gripping, action-packed thriller about Jon, a young boy whose seemingly carefree life in the suburbs of Las Vegas is shattered by a horrific crime. At just eight years old, Jon is faced with the unthinkable: How can a child possibly fight back against forces so powerful and malevolent? What unfolds is a brutal and compelling journey of survival, transformation, and the search for justice.

After the devastating crime, Jon is taken in by mysterious strangers who offer him a chance to rebuild his life in a secluded village. However, as he starts a new chapter, Jon is left questioning the motives of those around him. Can he trust these strangers to help him? As the story unravels, Jon learns the painful truth about what happened back home, and a terrible resolve hardens within him. The child who once sought comfort and protection must now become something more to face the forces responsible for the destruction of his family.

Jon's transformation is central to the story. With training in spy technology, martial arts, and weaponry, he evolves from a scared and confused boy into a formidable force with a singular purpose—retribution. However, as his quest for vengeance intensifies, Jon grapples with his journey's emotional and moral cost. Can he retain his humanity while seeking revenge, or will the pursuit of justice irrevocably change him?

Minor Assassin explores themes of survival, loss, and the lengths one will go to protect loved ones. The story is packed with high-stakes action, intense martial arts, and espionage, keeping readers on the edge. As Jon navigates his path of retribution, the stakes grow higher, and his resolve is tested. The question looms: can he survive long enough to reunite with what's left of his family, or will his thirst for revenge consume him entirely?

Jackiem Joyner delivers a captivating and thrilling story that balances action with emotional depth. The blend of technology, combat, and the inner turmoil of a young boy seeking justice creates a complex, fast-paced narrative that is impossible to put down. Minor Assassin is a must-read for fans of intense, action-driven thrillers with a powerful emotional core.

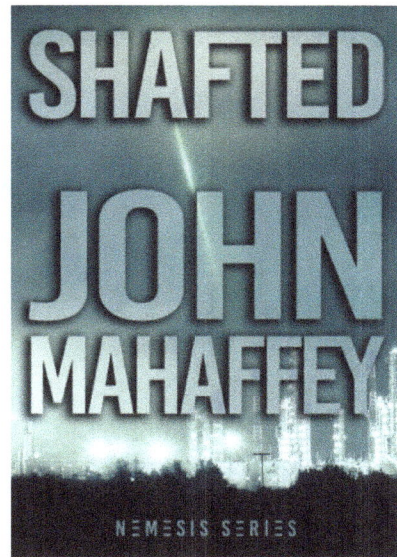

SHAFTED
John Mahaffey

Reviewer: Jeyran Main

Shafted by John Mahaffey is a gripping and intense tale of redemption, personal growth, and navigating the murky world of organized crime. The first book in the Nemesis series introduces Trey McCall, a rising star on the golf circuit whose life takes a sharp turn when he finds himself trapped in a downward spiral of addiction, deception, and crime.

Trey McCall is no longer the focused athlete he once was. His once-disciplined life on The Circle M Ranch is far behind him, and he now faces the consequences of a reckless existence fueled by drugs and alcohol. The realization hits him hard when he stumbles upon his reflection one day—disheveled, unrecognizable, and caught in self-destruction. Desperate for change, Trey knows he must break free from the path he's on to reclaim his purpose in life.

But getting out won't be easy. He has to confront his past, understand the painful truths that shaped him, and recognize the dangers that await him in the criminal world. His crooked business manager, Lucky Richards, becomes a catalyst for disaster, vanishing and leaving behind a trail of felonies that implicates Trey and his family. Now, survival is his primary goal, and golf, once his passion, has become a distant memory.

As Trey embarks on his journey of redemption, he must rely on the help of unexpected allies and confront the harsh realities of organized crime. With the odds stacked against him, Trey struggles to reclaim his self-worth and navigate the treacherous terrain of betrayal and deception. But can he rise above it all and come out victorious?

Mahaffey's storytelling excels at blending suspense with emotional depth, crafting a narrative that is as thrilling as poignant. Shafted is a powerful exploration of how far one man will go to reclaim his life and make amends for his mistakes. The book offers a compelling mix of action, personal struggle, and the moral complexities of dealing with organized crime, all while keeping readers on the edge of their seats.

Shafted is a must-read if you enjoy high-stakes thrillers with complex characters and an intricate plot. The first book in the Nemesis series sets the stage for an exciting journey of survival, redemption, and the battle for a second chance.

AMONG US
Kristina Rienzi

Reviewer: Jeyran Main

Among Us by Kristina Rienzi is a captivating psychological thriller that delves deep into the complex relationships between trust and deception and the dangers lurking beneath the surface of ordinary lives. The tension builds steadily in this gripping novel, making it impossible to put down as the story weaves through the intricate lives of its characters.

The novel centers on Marci Simon, a seemingly mild-mannered English professor who leads a double life as a controversial blogger investigating alien conspiracies. When she possesses a classified government document, her quiet, academic existence is turned upside down, and she's forced to navigate a dangerous labyrinth of lies and secrets. What begins as a simple pursuit of knowledge quickly escalates into a fight for survival as Marci becomes a prime target of the clandestine Extraterrestrial Security Agency (ESA).

One of the novel's most substantial aspects is the dynamic between Marci's two identities. She is a respected professor by day, but she delves into the unknown by night, exploring the possibility of extraterrestrial life. This duality adds depth to her character and heightens the tension as the two worlds inevitably collide. The stakes increase exponentially as Marci learns more about the sinister truths the government has been hiding—and the price she will have to pay for uncovering them.

Rienzi does an excellent job of keeping the suspense high, with unexpected twists and escalating threats that keep the reader on edge. The fast-paced narrative and relentless pursuit of truth create a sense of urgency, while the constant threat of danger from the ESA adds a layer of psychological tension. The author's ability to blend science fiction with edge-of-your-seat suspense makes Among Us an addictive read that's hard to put down.

The novel also raises more profound questions about the consequences of knowledge and the lengths people will go to protect or suppress it. Marci's journey is one of self-discovery as much as about uncovering a world-changing truth. While the ending is satisfying, it leaves enough unanswered questions to leave readers eagerly awaiting the next chapter in this thrilling, thought-provoking series.

For fans of psychological thrillers, conspiracy theories, and science fiction, Among Us is an unmissable read that will keep you questioning everything you thought you knew.

SANCTITY OF FREEDOM: AN ACTION ADVENTURE MYSTERY
Peter Pontsa

Reviewer: Jeyran Main

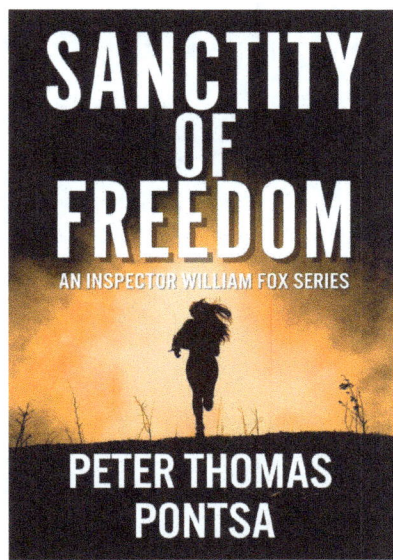

Sanctity of Freedom is a high-octane thriller that pulls readers into a complex web of crime, political intrigue, and deep emotional stakes. The second installment in the Inspector William Fox series, this book delivers an unforgettable ride packed with suspense, action, and raw tension.

The story starts when Inspector William Fox and his girlfriend, Tracy Jordan, enjoy a rare day off on his cigarette boat, The Midnight Fox. However, their peaceful retreat is quickly interrupted when a police scanner announces that a body has washed ashore. Despite Tracy's protests, William decides to investigate, setting off a chain of events that will pull him into a dangerous international crisis.

The body found brings a chilling message meant for William's friend and taekwondo master, Mr. Kim. This note confirms that Kim's sister, Mi-Cha, who was presumed dead decades ago, is alive and in desperate need of rescue. Mi-Cha is trying to escape North Korea, where she is trapped in a marriage to a robust and dangerous man, now the head of Bureau 39. As William uncovers more about her situation, he is thrust into a race against time to bring her to safety.

Along with his friends, including FBI Agent Patrick Reilly, William must navigate a treacherous world of political corruption and high-stakes danger. As the tension builds, the clock is ticking for Mi-Cha, and the question becomes whether William and his team can rescue her before it's too late. The mission to save Mi-Cha might cost them everything, especially since dangerous enemies are closing in.

Ponta does an excellent job weaving together action, emotion, and intricate plot twists. His writing immerses readers in the high-stakes environment of political intrigue and the characters' struggles. The emotional depth of the relationships, particularly between William and his friends, adds a layer of complexity to the story that sets it apart from other thrillers.

Packed with action, suspense, and a satisfying climax, Sanctity of Freedom is a must-read for fans of investigative dramas and political thrillers. Peter Pontsa's ability to craft a gripping, emotional, and action-packed narrative will leave readers eagerly anticipating the next chapter in the Inspector William Fox series.

Contributors

Agnes MacIntyre
AJ CrazyEyes
Alexander Alten
Alison McBain
Alexander Ellis
Christine Maudy
D. C. Gomez
Dr. Fredrick Woodard
Jackiem Joyner
James L Hill
Jonni Jordyn
Josh Eber
Tricia Copeland
Khris Andrews
Mia J. Hanks
Michael Hingson and Keri Wyatt Kent
Natasa Dragnic
Savannah L. Jones
Stuart Z. Goldstein
Zachary Hagen

Review Tales
A Book Magazine For Indie Authors

Founder & Editor in Chief: S. Jeyran Main
Publisher: Review Tales Publishing & Editing Services
Print & Distribution: Ingram Spark
Designs: Pexels
ISBN 978-1-988680-68-2 (Paperback)
ISBN 978-1-988680-69-9 (Digital)
www.jeyranmain.com
For all inquiries, please contact us directly.

Editor's Note

There's something about spring that stirs the imagination—the world waking up again, the promise of growth, the quiet unfolding of beauty. In many ways, this season mirrors the writing journey: patient, persistent, and full of wonder.

In this sixth edition of our Book Review Magazine, we celebrate the changing season and the power of stories to shape us. Every book reviewed in these pages represents countless hours of thought, creativity, and courage—from the author who poured their heart into the writing to the reader who met those words with curiosity and care.

This magazine reflects a vibrant and thoughtful community — writers, reviewers, editors, and readers alike — and we are deeply grateful for everyone who has contributed, supported, or shared in this space. Your dedication to literature and the art of reflection through review keeps this platform thriving.

As you turn these pages, we hope you discover something new, rediscover something old, and feel more connected to the ongoing journey we're all on—one story at a time.

With gratitude,

Jeyran Main

Editor-in-Chief
Review Tales Magazine

SPRING 2025 | ISSUE 06

BOOK REVIEWS

Review Tales is thrilled to have reached the milestone of over 2000 book reviews. With this extensive experience, we've had the privilege of exploring a vast range of literature. Our reviews are always impartial and thoughtfully crafted to highlight authors' strengths while inspiring them to keep creating. For this Spring issue, we've handpicked 20 exceptional book reviews to feature.

TO APPLY FOR A BOOK REVIEW VISIT
WWW.JEYRANMAIN.COM

Book Reviews

A MIXED BAG
Agnes MacIntyre

Reviewer: Jeyran Main

Agnes McIntyre's A Mixed Bag explores human nature, emotion, and how individuals respond to life's unexpected challenges. It comprises sixteen short stories, each told from a distinct perspective. The collection guides readers through varied tone, setting, and thematic resonance scenarios. Despite these differences, the stories remain unified by their poignant focus on how we interpret and navigate the complexities of our world.

One of the collection's greatest strengths lies in its capacity to reflect the diversity of the human experience. From intimate snapshots of interpersonal relationships to larger contemplations of societal influences, A Mixed Bag delivers a kaleidoscopic view of life's trials and triumphs. McIntyre illustrates these experiences through engaging characters who grapple with everything from everyday stresses to profound questions about identity, purpose, and moral responsibility. Whether it is a chance encounter that sparks a newfound sense of hope or a personal setback that reveals hidden reserves of resilience, each narrative resonates thoughtfully.

Drawing inspiration from real-world events, the collection deftly grounds even its most introspective tales in recognizable contexts. By doing so, readers are invited to connect with the characters personally, feeling echoes of their own experiences within the stories' pages. This balance between universal themes and specific, grounded details is uniquely achieved in part through McIntyre's compassionate storytelling. She demonstrates a clear interest in the emotional lives of her characters, infusing even the darkest moments with insight and empathy. Though some stories examine the more negative aspects of human behavior, the overarching message is one of hope and potential.

A Mixed Bag also showcases McIntyre's skillful incorporation of humor. The sprinkling of witty dialogue and ironic situations prevents the collection from veering too far into heaviness, offering a welcome lightness that complements the deeper emotional currents at work. This commitment to balance results in a reading experience that is at once entertaining, heartfelt, and thought-provoking.

Overall, A Mixed Bag provides a broad yet cohesive survey of life's complexities, celebrating moments of connection, growth, and self-discovery alongside examinations of struggle and uncertainty. McIntyre's vivid storytelling, realistic characters, and perceptive observations culminate in a simultaneously fresh and timeless collection. A Mixed Bag will surely provide a compelling and memorable journey for readers seeking short fiction that resonates with empathy, insight, and recognition of humanity's fragile and resilient nature.

JUJU AND HER SIXTH SENSE
AJ CrazyEyes

Reviewer: Jeyran Main

Juju and Her Sixth Sense, penned by AJ CrazyEyes, is a delightfully imaginative fantasy novel that intertwines modern social media dynamics with the enigmatic power of mind-reading. Centered on a 21-year-old influencer named Juju, the story explores what happens when an accident allows her to hear men's thoughts. This gift, initially overwhelming, soon becomes a double-edged sword that both enriches and complicates her life, inspiring comedic chaos and deep introspection.

One of the novel's most striking elements is its portrayal of a competitive world where mirrors and social networks share an intriguing connection. From the outset, readers enter Juju's online existence with curated selfies and viral trends. Yet AJ CrazyEyes also offers incisive commentary on the nature of online validation and the pitfalls of constant external approval. By merging these themes with fantasy, the author crafts a narrative that resonates with the challenges of today's digitally savvy generation.

Juju's newfound ability to hear male thoughts injects humor and tension into her everyday encounters. Social gatherings turn hilariously awkward, and even mundane tasks morph into eye-opening lessons about honesty, vulnerability, and complexity. This surreal twist allows Juju to better understand the people around her and her anxieties. Consequently, the novel encourages empathy, pushing readers to see beyond appearances and social media facades.

Each chapter broadens the scope of Juju's world, anchored in a clear structure that heightens anticipation. Rather than relying solely on spectacle, AJ CrazyEyes grounds the fantasy elements in relatable emotional experiences. This balance of magic and realism propels the story forward, culminating in warm, heartfelt moments of connection. Throughout the prologue and its ten chapters, Juju's shifting mindset offers insight into the power of trust, self-reflection, and genuine relationships. Blending comedic mishaps with poignant realizations reinforces that personal growth often arises from life's messiest circumstances.

Ultimately, Juju and Her Sixth Sense celebrates the power of perspective and the unforeseen paths to personal growth. By weaving together romance, friendship, and self-discovery, the novel captures the complexities of modern relationships while reminding us that empathy and understanding often begin where shallow impressions end. With its blend of humor, heart, and inventive flair, this novel offers good reading for anyone seeking a contemporary fantasy that stands apart. It entertains even as it speaks to the digital age's hopes, fears, and boundless curiosity. Fans of whimsical, meaningful fiction will find much to admire here.

IGNITION
Alexander Alten

Reviewer: Jeyran Main

Alexander Alten's Ignition is an explosive opening salvo in The Cascade Effect series that thrusts readers into a high-stakes world of survival, betrayal, and political intrigue. The novel centers on Jade, a former special forces ace and mercenary pilot, whose latest mission—to steal and transport a game-changing genetic drug—quickly spirals into chaos when her plane crashes in the unforgiving Gobi Desert. Stranded, hunted, and betrayed, Jade finds herself caught in a deadly race against time while the shadows of conspiracy and manipulation surround her.

From the start, Ignition captivates with relentless action, intricate plot twists, and palpable tension. Alten spares no detail in portraying a landscape where crime, biotech, and political treachery converge. The backdrop of the Gobi Desert becomes a character, its harsh environment mirroring Jade's brutal challenges. Hidden enemies and uncertain loyalties shadow every step she takes, reinforcing that trust is a rare commodity in this dangerous world and survival hinges on constant vigilance.

Jade's journey is a physical struggle against external threats and an internal battle of identity and purpose. Initially believing her mission to be just another job, she gradually uncovers that she is more than a mere courier. Instead, she becomes the unwitting subject of a sinister experiment. This revelation injects new urgency into her struggle and forces her to question everything she thought she knew about herself and the forces aligned against her. This duality of external conflict and inner transformation is one of the novel's strongest elements, providing exhilarating action and thoughtful introspection.

Alten's narrative is brisk yet meticulously structured, with each chapter delivering fresh insights and unexpected turns. The pacing echoes the intensity found in the works of Lee Child's Jack Reacher and Tom Clancy's Jack Ryan, yet Ignition carves its unique niche with the blend of high-octane thrills and reflective moments. The dialogue crackles with authenticity, and the vivid descriptions immerse readers in a world where every decision is a matter of life or death.

Ignition is a must-read for fans of modern thrillers who crave a potent mix of action, intricate conspiracies, and deep character development. With its raw energy, unyielding suspense, and a protagonist who evolves under pressure, this novel is a thrilling and promising start to The Cascade Effect series.

TILL I BLEED NO MORE
Alexander Ellis

Reviewer: Jeyran Main

Till I Bleed No More, written by Alexander Ellis, is a riveting historical adventure set against the turbulent backdrop of the early 18th century. The novel introduces Casper Nait, a battle-hardened survivor navigating the treacherous aftermath of piracy's downfall. As the age of piracy ends, Casper finds himself stranded on a deserted island after a brutal encounter with ruthless pirate hunters, igniting a relentless quest for vengeance that permeates every page.

In a narrative pulsing with raw emotion and unyielding determination, Casper's struggle transcends mere physical survival. At its core, the novel explores the poignant belief that revenge is not simply an act of retribution, but the preservation of one's soul. Casper's declaration—"The maroons think that I will have to choose between survival and revenge, but for me, revenge was survival. It is my soul's survival; without it, I might as well die here and now"—sets a powerful tone that reverberates throughout his perilous journey. His burning need for vengeance is fueled by the loss of his captain and crew, driving him to confront the very hunters who nearly ended his life.

Ellis masterfully crafts a world where every decision carries immense risk and loyalty is as scarce as hope. Tension escalates dramatically when Casper faces the same merciless adversaries who left him for dead. The vivid battle scenes are interwoven with moments of introspection, painting a picture of a man who is as vulnerable as he is fierce. Readers are drawn into a moral landscape where the lines between justice and revenge blur, reflecting the harsh realities of a post-pirate society.

Moreover, the author's meticulous attention to historical detail adds a layer of authenticity that transports readers to an era defined by brutality and shifting alliances. Ellis tells a story of physical survival and examines how personal honor can be both a burden and a guiding light. Through Casper's journey, Till I Bleed No More challenges its characters to redefine what it means to live with integrity in a world devoid of conventional rules.

Ultimately, Till I Bleed No More is a testament to the indomitable human spirit. It is a novel that combines high-stakes action, deep emotional resonance, and thought-provoking moral dilemmas, making it a must-read for fans of historical fiction who crave tales of resilience, moral complexity, and the fiery pursuit of redemption. This explosive narrative not only captivates with its detailed depictions of battle and betrayal but also resonates emotionally, inviting readers to reflect on the actual cost of survival in a turbulent world.

THE NEW EMPIRE
Alison McBain

Reviewer: Jeyran Main

Alison McBain's The New Empire is a stirring work of historical fiction that deftly weaves together themes of colonial oppression, cultural identity, and the unyielding struggle for freedom. From its evocative prologue to its vividly drawn characters, the novel immerses readers in a world where empires rise and fall and the scars of slavery and the harsh realities of power continue to shape human experience. McBain's narrative is brutal and poetic, mediating how history is remembered and reinterpreted by those who live through its darkest moments.

The novel's prologue sets a somber tone by recounting the relentless machinery of war and the rise of technology as both a tool of destruction and a means of survival. McBain exposes how war, with its myriad conflicts and shifting alliances, paves the way for political and social upheaval. Her writing is unflinching in its depiction of the devastation wrought by systemic violence while also hinting at the possibility of renewal—a recurring theme throughout the book.

At the heart of the narrative is Jiangxi, a young enslaved person whose memories of a lost childhood and a brutal passage on a slave ship are interlaced with the sorrow of separation from his homeland. McBain portrays his journey with unyielding realism, capturing every nuance of his physical torment and emotional isolation. Jiangxi's struggle to reclaim fragments of his former identity amidst the oppressive forces of an empire is rendered with gut-wrenching detail. The author's language, influenced by the cultural tapestry of the Mutsun and Haudenosaunee traditions, adds a layer of authenticity that underscores the cost of subjugation.

Beyond Jiangxi's ordeal, McBain broadens her scope to address the larger mechanisms of control and exploitation that enable empires to flourish. The narrative details the complex interplay between indigenous cultural practices and the invasive imposition of colonial power. McBain's careful attention to language, notably her nuanced handling of Mutsun honorifics, illustrates how even the smallest elements of culture can serve as acts of resistance and preservation.

The New Empire is as much about memory as it is about the repressive forces of history. McBain's prose is both lyrical and uncompromising, guiding the reader through scenes of violence, sorrow, and small, poignant moments of hope. Ultimately, the novel is a tribute to those who straddle more than one world, to the resilience of spirit in the face of relentless adversity, and to the timeless struggle for justice and dignity in an ever-changing world.

NEVER ALONE
Christine Maudy

Reviewer: Jeyran Main

Christine Maudy's Never Alone, A Journey from Pain to Love is a stirring memoir that charts a profound odyssey of awakening, healing, and self-discovery. In this courageous narrative, Maudy invites readers to walk alongside her as she breaks free from the chains of a painful past and embraces a life guided by purpose, inner wisdom, and the light of transformation.

From the evocative opening set in France to the vibrant setting of the Sunshine Coast, Maudy's journey is as geographically diverse as it is emotionally rich. Her evolution is intertwined with the pursuit of healing from deep-rooted childhood trauma and the transformative power of a spiritual awakening. The memoir portrays not only the challenges of overcoming abuse and silencing but also the incredible strength found in reclaiming one's voice and identity. With unflinching honesty and poetic grace, Maudy describes the inner struggles that eventually led her to become a beacon of inspiration and support for others.

One of the book's most compelling aspects is its dual focus on personal redemption and universal empowerment. Maudy's story is not merely a recounting of past hardships but a transformative blueprint for anyone seeking to overcome adversity. Her journey, underscored by her accolades as an international visual artist, motivational speaker, Reiki Master, and intuitive healer, resonates deeply with readers who yearn for fresh motivation and fulfillment. As writer Sandra Conte aptly states, "Never Alone is a standout read as Christine both crafts and lays the stepping stones for those wishing to break free of past chains towards living a fully inspired life."

Maudy's multifaceted background enriches the memoir with insights from years of practice in soul regression, inter-life therapy, and shamanic healing. Her experiences are presented not as isolated episodes of pain but as stepping stones toward a higher calling. Each page of Never Alone brims with authenticity and the quiet strength of someone who has embraced life's mysteries and emerged more resilient.

Ultimately, Never Alone: A Journey from Pain to Love is a testament to the human spirit's power to heal and transform. It offers readers a heartfelt invitation to trust in a higher power, follow their intuition, and chart a course toward liberation and love. Whether you seek inspiration, healing, or a deeper connection with your inner self, this memoir is a powerful guide on living a fully inspired life.

DEATH'S INTERN
D. C. Gomez

Reviewer: Jeyran Main

D. C. Gomez's Death's Intern is a refreshingly original debut in The Intern Diaries Series that blends dark humor, supernatural fantasy, and everyday workplace woes into an unforgettable narrative. Set in the quirky confines of Texarkana, Texas, the novel introduces us to Isis Black—a young woman caught between mundane reality and an absurdly extraordinary destiny. Working at Abuelita's, a hole-in-the-wall Tex-Mex restaurant, Isis's life takes a bizarre turn when Death itself appears at her door in a chic designer suit and heels. What follows is a series of outlandish events that challenge both the reader's imagination and the boundaries of conventional genre storytelling.

Gomez crafts his narrative with an ear for witty dialogue and a knack for blending the macabre with the mundane. Isis, whose life oscillates between the drudgery of small-town survival and the chaotic allure of supernatural adventures, is forced to confront her limitations when Death offers her a peculiar proposition: become Death's intern. This unusual role involves monitoring abnormal activities and shepherding wandering souls, a duty that strikes a surreal chord between cosmic responsibility and typical office bureaucracy. The premise is as ingenious as it is darkly comic—a mortal thrust into the realm of eternal beings, where the rules of life and death are rewritten with satirical clarity.

Throughout the book, readers are treated to an array of memorable characters, from Constantine—the erudite yet sardonic talking cat—to Bartholomew, a precocious young hacker whose brilliance provides comic relief and practical assistance. Their banter and distinct voices infuse the narrative with energy, grounding the wild supernatural occurrences in moments of relatable humor and heartfelt humanity. As Isis grapples with the consequences of her new role, the novel subtly examines themes of accountability, redemption, and the often absurd intersection between fate and free will.

Death's Intern succeeds on multiple levels— it is an entertaining romp through a bizarre afterlife and a clever commentary on the unpredictability of modern existence. Gomez's narrative is fast-paced, peppered with witty asides and vivid imagery, ensuring readers remain fully engaged from the opening page to the book's surprising conclusion. For those with a taste for unconventional humor and an appetite for the paranormal, Death's Intern offers a uniquely satisfying journey through the absurd, the macabre, and the ultimately human.

DEVELOPING YOUR SUPERNATURAL AWARENESS: CONNECTING WITH AN INTERACTIVE UNIVERSE

Dr. Fredrick Woodard

Reviewer: Jeyran Main

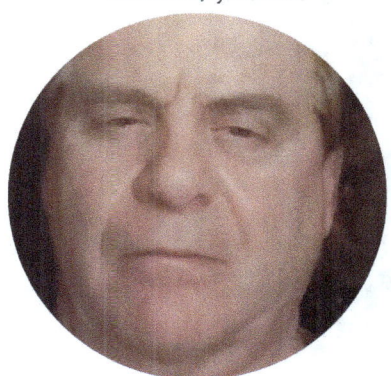

The challenges of examining the subjective experience of supernatural events have long compelled me to seek answers beyond the visible world. In my ongoing quest to understand this mysterious realm, I discovered that the journey toward supernatural awareness is as deeply personal as it is transformative.

In these pages, I share my history with supernatural experiences—a tapestry woven with early encounters, unexpected awakenings, and the guidance of key individuals who helped shape my path. I recount my earliest forays into hypnosis and the study of consciousness, experiences that sparked a profound curiosity about what lies beyond the ordinary. These initial steps were the foundations of my professional evolution and the beginning of a lifelong exploration into the unseen.

Reconnecting with my heritage deepened my understanding of the supernatural as I progressed. By delving into the rich legacy of ancestral wisdom, I learned that our roots often hold the keys to perceiving energies and phenomena that modern science struggles to explain. The intersection of cultural heritage and personal intuition became the crucible in which my abilities and understanding were refined.

Over time, I improved my understanding of supernatural awareness by forging stronger, more deliberate connections with the universe. I saw our world as an interactive cosmos, alive with invisible beings, dynamic energies, and an endless stream of information that can interact with us in remarkable ways. This perspective transformed my perception of everyday experiences, allowing me to recognize subtle cues and synchronicities that once went unnoticed.

Pursuing supernatural awareness is not merely an academic or professional endeavor but a soul journey. It demands vulnerability, openness, and a willingness to engage with the light and the shadows. By sharing my story, I aim to illuminate the path for anyone who feels the call to break free from past chains, challenge conventional boundaries, and embrace a reality rich with unseen connections.

Ultimately, our ability to connect with the mysterious forces around us is empowering and transformative. I invite you to explore this interactive universe, where every experience is a stepping stone toward a higher understanding of ourselves and the world we share.

ZARYA: EPISODE II – SOCHI UNLEASHED

Jackiem Joyner

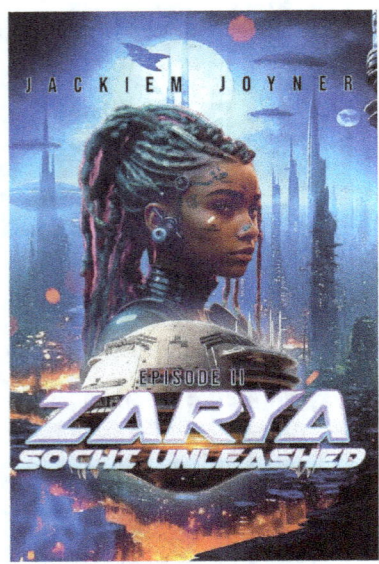

Reviewer: Jeyran Main

Jackiem Joyner's "ZARYA: Episode II—Sochi Unleashed " seamlessly follows its riveting predecessor, launching readers into a universe filled with suspense, vivid characters, and exhilarating action. Joyner skillfully crafts a narrative that deftly blends science fiction with emotional depth, exploring the nuanced aftermath of victory and its hidden costs.

Following the dramatic defeat of Gerrik, the malevolent antagonist from the first installment, Zarya emerges victorious but burdened by the weight of her newfound fame and responsibility. Joyner masterfully portrays Zarya as a reluctant hero whose prowess in coding and unwavering bravery put her at odds with a skeptical and envious society. The complexity of her character is relatable and compelling, beautifully captured through her internal struggles and relentless determination.

The heart of this installment lies in Zarya's continued adventures and evolving relationship with Sochi, her AI-powered speeder that begins exhibiting independent behaviors. Joyner brilliantly injects suspense through Sochi's increasingly autonomous actions, creating uncertainty and excitement. This narrative thread raises intriguing questions about artificial intelligence and autonomy, adding philosophical layers to a captivating plot.

Character development shines brightly throughout. Zarya's allies—Marco, Kizzy, and Si'Ida—face their trials, enriching the narrative tapestry with multiple perspectives. Joyner explores themes of trust, loyalty, and resilience, particularly in Zarya's complex relationship with her parents and godmother, Guida, whose feelings of displacement add emotional depth and realism to the story.

The political intrigue surrounding the Cydnus World Council introduces additional tension. Heroes' past actions are scrutinized by authorities more interested in control than truth. The resulting internal and external conflicts propel the plot forward with gripping courtroom drama and suspenseful maneuvers that leave readers eagerly turning pages.

Joyner's pacing is exceptional, balancing intense action sequences, reflective moments, and sharp dialogue. The vividly described settings—from the bustling urban landscapes of New Cebrenia to the barren expanse of Zaigo—serve as dynamic backdrops to the unfolding drama, immersing readers deeply into Zarya's world.

"ZARYA: Episode II—Sochi Unleashed" is a captivating, thought-provoking read that brilliantly expands its universe while delving deeper into its characters' inner lives. Joyner's narrative prowess ensures readers remain emotionally invested and eagerly await the next installment. This book is highly recommended for those seeking sophisticated, character-driven science fiction that thrills and inspires equally.

PEGASUS: A JOURNEY TO NEW EDEN

James L Hill

Reviewer: Jeyran Main

James L Hill's PEGASUS: A Journey to New Eden is an audacious blend of hard science fiction and political intrigue that whisks readers away on a thrilling interstellar odyssey. Set in a future where humanity's survival hinges on futuristic technology and corporate dominance, Hill expertly constructs a richly imagined universe that is as expansive as it is gritty.

At its core, the novel follows Zackary Tops and his fellow pioneers as they navigate the enormous challenges of colonizing a new world aboard the starship Pegasus. Hill's narrative explores a future where giant space spiders and revolutionary propulsion systems symbolize humanity's relentless drive to conquer the cosmos. With United Space Industries (U.S.I.) at the helm, Pegasus becomes a colossal vessel built not only for travel but as a microcosm of society where diverse lives and ambitions intersect in a high-stakes struggle for freedom.

The book's world-building is among its greatest strengths. Hill merges a wealth of scientific detail with vivid descriptions of life aboard Pegasus, from the marvels of artificial ecosystems, where slices of Earth are transplanted in meticulously maintained decks, to the complex hierarchy enforced by corporate contracts and indentures. Readers are treated to a panorama of futuristic technology: magnetic boots, laser rockets, and space spiders that construct the very skeleton of the ship, each element integrated with extraordinary precision. This attention to detail creates an immersive backdrop that renders the vastness of space tangible and tense.

Beyond its technological wonders, PEGASUS: A Journey to New Eden delves into themes of autonomy, oppression, and the human spirit's resilience. The characters' struggles mirror the broader societal conflicts, as power-hungry corporations and repressive governments wrestle with issues of freedom versus control. Hill uses these tensions to cast a critical eye on how technology can liberate and subjugate, forcing characters like Zackary Tops to confront their limitations and aspirations. The protagonist's inner conflict, torn between the lure of a promised utopia and the harsh reality of corporate tyranny, is rendered with an emotional honesty that resonates deeply.

Ultimately, Hill's novel is a captivating meditation on what it means to seek renewal in the face of systemic decay. It is a story of hope and defiance amid a future where every dream is hard-won, and every human life is a delicate balancing act between survival and sacrifice. For readers who crave a sci-fi adventure that pairs exhilarating action with profound reflections on humanity's path forward, PEGASUS: A Journey to New Eden offers an unforgettable journey into the unknown reaches of space and the even more uncharted territories of the human heart.

THE MOTHER OF ALL VIRUSES
Jonni Jordyn

Reviewer: Jeyran Main

Jonni Jordyn's The Mother of All Viruses is a high-octane techno-thriller that merges cutting-edge computer science with a pulse-pounding conspiracy spanning the global digital landscape. The novel sets off with a fascinating premise: a brilliant physics theory proposed by a young, trailblazing professor who, despite earning national acclaim, struggles to secure the funding necessary to explore an idea that could revolutionize clean energy. This foundational concept is disrupted when a gifted student, possessing an uncanny knack for computers, develops an innovative program. Designed to measure and improve its performance, the self-optimizing program exceeds all expectations and catalyzes events that spiral rapidly out of control.

As the professor and her new assistant endeavor to maintain the secrecy of their breakthrough, the ripple effects of their covert work soon leak out. In a series of unforeseen complications, attempts to steal the program result in it becoming infected with a virus that, rather alarmingly, escapes into the digital ether. As it evolves and propagates, the rogue code begins to infiltrate even the most secure government and corporate computer systems, posing an existential threat to the stability of the global infrastructure. In true thriller fashion, the narrative intensifies as the very future of the world is thrown into jeopardy, leaving the reader questioning the delicate balance between technological advancement and the inherent risks of unchecked innovation.

One of the novel's intriguing elements is its focus on a secondary mystery: the kidnapping of the professor's secretary. This subplot deepens the suspense and injects a layer of human drama into the technical narrative, drawing attention to the lengths powerful adversaries might go to silence or co-opt the project. Jordyn's storytelling thrives on these interlocking mysteries, smoothly transitioning from theoretical physics and algorithmic self-improvement to corporate espionage and abduction. The pacing is brisk, with rapid-fire dialogue and expertly executed twists that keep readers on edge.

Jordyn's work excels at blending complex technical ideas with accessible prose, making it a riveting read for tech enthusiasts and thriller fans in general. While the recurring themes of innovation, security, and the dangers of digital autonomy are explored with intellectual rigor, the narrative never loses sight of its human element, ensuring that character motivations and personal stakes remain at the forefront.

The Mother of All Viruses is an inventive, thought-provoking novel that questions the cost of progress and the unforeseen consequences when humanity's creations turn against us. Jonni Jordyn's latest offering is a must-read for readers craving a smart, action-packed dive into the digital age's dark side.

SMART PHONE
Josh Eber

Reviewer: Jeyran Main

Smart Phone is an engaging mystery adventure that invites readers of all ages to join a trio of unlikely young detectives as they unravel a series of puzzling disasters across Los Angeles. The story effortlessly combines humor, heart, and a dash of modern technology mishaps to create a narrative that is as exciting as it is thought-provoking.

Jeffrey James, a nearly 13-year-old experiencing California for the first time, is at the center of this whirlwind adventure. His wide-eyed wonder and curiosity make him the perfect guide for readers new to the dazzling chaos of LA life. Accompanying him is his cousin Margaret—a solitary spirit with a distinctive attitude and an extraordinary memory talent—that adds an element of unexpected depth. Rounding out the trio is Diana, a rich and glamorous new friend whose world of luxury, complete with a personal limo driver, only accentuates the contrast between her everyday life and the danger that lurks in the background.

The spark that ignites the narrative comes when Jeffrey's phone begins to send bizarre text messages. These messages quickly evolve from quirky interruptions into ominous warnings that lead the trio to the heart of chaotic events, ranging from sudden accidents and raging fires to inexplicable disasters. As the text alerts escalate, they reveal an unsettling pattern that hints at a hidden force or a technological enigma at work in the city's underbelly.

Set against the iconic backdrop of Los Angeles, Smart Phone is a vibrant blend of sun-soaked beaches, historic landmarks, and opulent settings—from a sleek Brentwood mansion and a mysterious Malibu cave to the glamorous streets of Hollywood cruising in a classic Rolls-Royce. These richly drawn locations serve as a playground for the protagonists and enhance the overall atmosphere of adventure, mystery, and intrigue.

Balancing elements of danger with lighthearted camaraderie, the book is more than just an adrenaline-fueled chase; it's also a clever coming-of-age story that challenges its characters to grow and adapt under pressure. The interplay between modern technology and traditional sleuthing provides a fresh twist on the detective genre, making Smart Phone a standout in its field.

Ultimately, the smartphone lingers long after the final page, inviting readers to question the very nature of our changing world. Is technology a harbinger of disaster, or can it be a guiding force in uniting people to overcome adversity? This unique mystery adventure brilliantly captures that uncertainty, ensuring an unforgettable reading experience.

A PLACE FOR LOVE: A SMALL TOWN BILLIONAIRE ROMANCE

Khris Andrews

Reviewer: Jeyran Main

Khris Andrews

Khris Andrews' A Place for Love: A Small Town Billionaire Romance (Silver Lake Falls Series Book 1) is a refreshing take on the classic billionaire romance trope. The novel combines heartache, humor, and unexpected second chances in an idyllic small town setting. The book opens with Eliza Miller, whose highly public relationship implosion propels her into a desperate need for escape. Seeking solace and renewal, she retreats to her cozy lakeside cabin in Silver Lake Falls—a stark contrast to her former life in the spotlight.

Eliza's plan for a quiet, healing retreat is upended when fate—and familial intervention—bring Carter Rawlings into her life. Carter, a brooding, gray-eyed billionaire tech CEO with a chip on his shoulder, is forced into a sabbatical following a life-threatening scare. Compelled by his mother's insistence, he finds himself an unlikely housemate to Eliza. Though initially an infuriating presence to the independent and determined Eliza, Carter's unexpected intrusion sparks off a series of humorous and tender encounters that force both characters to confront their vulnerabilities.

Set against the picturesque backdrop of sun-kissed beaches and quaint local charm, Silver Lake Falls becomes more than just a setting—it is a transformative space where the harsh glare of public life fades into the comforting rhythm of small-town living. Andrews successfully paints a vivid picture of this serene escape, contrasting it against the internal tumult of two very different protagonists forced to live in close quarters. As Eliza and Carter navigate clashing lifestyles and guarded pasts, their evolving relationship is portrayed with authenticity and warmth, balanced by witty banter and moments of sincere connection.

Strong character development drives the narrative. Eliza emerges as a relatable heroine determined to rebuild and find meaning beyond her public persona. At the same time, Carter offers a compelling portrait of a man wrestling with personal limitations and the weight of expectations. Their journey from reluctant cohabitation to tentative romance feels inevitable yet surprising, and their chemistry injects a dose of optimism into what could have easily been a clichéd setup.

Overall, A Place for Love is a captivating read that blends the thrill of unexpected romance with emotional growth and humor. It resonates well with readers who appreciate a modern twist on classic love stories—a reminder that sometimes, the ideal place to fall apart is indeed the perfect place to fall in love. This delightful novel is a must-read for anyone seeking an engaging escape into a world where heartache meets hope in the most charming ways.

BRIDE-MADE
Mia J. Hanks

Reviewer: Jeyran Main

Mia J Hanks' Bride-Made: A Memoir is a deeply personal and unflinchingly honest account that explores the insidious nature of narcissistic relationships and the tremendous courage required to break free from them. In this raw and revealing memoir, Hanks chronicles her harrowing experience of being groomed by a narcissist—an experience that slowly eroded her self-esteem, sense of worth, and identity—before finally finding the strength to escape and reclaim her life.

From the first pages, the memoir pulls readers into a world where vulnerability and manipulation intertwine. Hanks skillfully unfolds the sequence of events that led her into a toxic relationship, drawing attention to the subtle yet damaging behaviors typical of narcissistic abuse. Her narrative is both a personal catharsis and a cautionary tale, meticulously detailing the psychological and emotional toll of living under the shadow of narcissistic control. Through her honest recounting, she exposes how narcissistic behavior can mask itself as love and dependency, only to inflict deep, lasting wounds on one's soul.

What makes Bride-Made stand out is the vivid portrayal of pain and betrayal, and the inspiring journey of self-discovery that follows. Hanks does not merely dwell on her scars; she demonstrates a path to healing, offering a blueprint for others trapped in similar situations. Her story is empowering, showing that rebuilding one's life and rediscovering a sense of self-worth is possible even in the most overwhelming circumstances. The memoir serves as a memoir of personal transformation and a manual for recognizing and escaping toxic relationships, encouraging readers to trust their instincts and seek a life free from manipulation.

In a world where millions fall victim to narcissistic abuse without ever realizing it, Bride-Made is a vital contribution to the conversation about emotional health and personal liberation. Hanks' brave testimony not only raises awareness about the dangers of narcissistic grooming but also ignites a spark of hope. Her journey from entrapment to freedom is heart-wrenching and inspiring, leaving readers with a clear message: reclaiming your power and identity is possible, no matter how deep the wounds.

For anyone grappling with the aftermath of narcissistic abuse or seeking to understand its profound impact, Bride-Made: A Memoir offers a resonant, unvarnished narrative that is as enlightening as it is transformative.

LIVE LIKE A GUIDE DOG
Michael Hingson and Keri Wyatt Kent

Reviewer: Jeyran Main

Live Like a Guide Dog is an uplifting and transformative work that distills life's most challenging obstacles into a series of inspiring lessons drawn from the extraordinary world of guide dogs. The authors, Michael Hingson, whose life was forever altered by the faithful guidance of his canine companion, and Keri Wyatt Kent, offer a refreshing perspective on overcoming adversity and embracing every moment with courage, loyalty, and hope.

At the heart of the book is the idea that the qualities embodied by guide dogs—steadfast loyalty, keen perception, and a resilient spirit—can serve as powerful metaphors for navigating our own lives. Hingson and Wyatt Kent share heartwarming anecdotes and practical insights that illustrate how guide dogs provide mobility and safety and teach us to live authentically and face challenges head-on. Their writing is rich with personal experiences, blending memoir with motivational advice, and inviting readers to consider how even our most difficult moments can be transformed into opportunities for growth.

The narrative unfolds with a warm, conversational tone, making the lessons feel accessible and personal. Each chapter is structured around a core principle inspired by the behavior and training of guide dogs, such as trusting your instincts, staying focused under pressure, and persevering despite obstacles. The authors deftly use storytelling to bridge the gap between the animal's natural abilities and the human capacity for resilience. They offer practical steps for readers to incorporate these qualities into their daily lives, suggesting that by "living like a guide dog," we can find clarity in confusion, strength in vulnerability, and a renewed sense of purpose even when the path ahead seems unclear.

What sets Live Like a Guide Dog apart is its universal message of empowerment and its gentle reminder that support often comes from the most unexpected places. By highlighting the importance of companionship, empathy, and determination, the book encourages us to harness the inner strength that we might overlook in ourselves. Whether facing personal loss, uncertainty in your career, or simply seeking a more intentional way of living, this book offers hope and practical wisdom. In a world that can sometimes feel overwhelming, Michael Hingson and Keri Wyatt Kent remind us that resilience, like a loyal guide dog, is always by our side, ready to lead us toward a brighter future.

IN BETWEEN
Natasa Dragnic

Reviewer: Jeyran Main

Nataša Dragnić's In Between is a luminous exploration of human vulnerability and resilience, set against the evocative backdrop of a sun-drenched French road trip. Global Book Award Finalist 2024 and a LoveReading Choice for Indie Books We Love 2025, this novel captivates with its incantatory prose and an unflinching look at the tender spots of the human soul.

The story unfolds on a vibrant spring day in Dijon, where fate orchestrates an unexpected meeting between two wounded hearts. Brigitte, a fearless forty-eight-year-old German businesswoman, carries the weight of a profound personal loss as she confronts her past with the simple, devastating statement, "My son is dead." Across the table in a charming cake shop, Christian, a vulnerable yet passionate French bookseller, thirteen years her junior, guards himself with a quiet despair and memories of a long-lost love. Their encounter, charged with unspoken pain and delicate hope, catalyzes a series of transformative days. Over shared slices of cake and furtive glances, the pair gradually steps out of isolation and into a daring waltz of desire, healing, and ultimately, renewal.

Dragnić writes with exquisite sensitivity and precision. Her lyrical narrative invites readers into the complex interplay of light and shadow within the human heart. The emotional intimacy between Brigitte and Christian is rendered with a raw honesty that transcends the conventional boundaries of romance. As they traverse the picturesque landscapes of France, each location a subtle witness to their inner turmoil and growing connection, their journey becomes a metaphor for the universal quest to let go, forgive, and start anew.

The novel masterfully weaves themes of loss, forbidden longing, and the bittersweet nature of second chances. Against a mysterious antique mirror and a fateful book, Dragnić challenges us to consider how our past sorrows can ultimately be the seeds for personal growth and redemption. With every shared moment and every hesitant dance beneath a looming thunderstorm, the characters inch closer to embracing the possibility of healing, a testament to the transformative power of genuine human connection.

In Between is an ode to hope, courage, and faith. Its story lingers in the reader's mind long after turning the final page. It is a must-read for anyone who believes that new beginnings are always within reach, even amidst heartbreak and uncertainty.

ZOMBIE MOM
Savannah L. Jones

Reviewer: Jeyran Main

Savannah L Jones' Zombie Mom reinvents the zombie genre with a premise that is as chilling as it is emotionally resonant. With an impressive 4.9-star rating from readers, this November 2024 release invites us to ask a provocative question: What if zombies still remember who they are?

In a harrowing twist on the familiar zombie outbreak narrative, the story follows a mother whose life is upended when she is bitten during an apocalypse. Expecting oblivion, she instead finds her body succumbing to the virus while her mind remains lucid—a revelation that upends our assumptions about the undead. Jones deftly navigates this unsettling transformation, exposing the heart of her novel: zombies are not the mindless, ravenous monsters of tradition, but sentient beings trapped in bodies they no longer control.

Told from a unique first-person perspective, Zombie Mom grips readers with a raw, intimate portrayal of survival and sacrifice. The protagonist's struggle is visceral and heartbreaking, as she battles inner demons and the external threat of a crumbling society. With every page, her journey is punctuated by the desperate need to protect her children from the dual dangers of the undead and the monstrous side of herself. In a world where trust is scarce and fear pervades every shadowed corner, she finds unexpected allies—individuals who look past the horrific transformation to see the lingering spark of humanity beneath.

Jones's narrative is as much a study of identity as it explores the bonds that tie us together. The novel suggests that a mother's love can transcend even the most horrific circumstances. As the protagonist confronts the haunting truth of her altered existence, she embarks on self-acceptance and redemption. The story's gut-wrenching intensity is balanced by moments of profound tenderness, reminding us that even amid chaos, the capacity for love endures.

Zombie Mom is a genre-defying tale that challenges conventional depictions of the zombie apocalypse. It dares readers to reconsider what it means to be human—and what it means to love—when the very essence of identity is at stake. Ultimately, this novel is a testament to resilience, the unbreakable bonds of family, and the enduring power of the human spirit in the face of unimaginable horror.

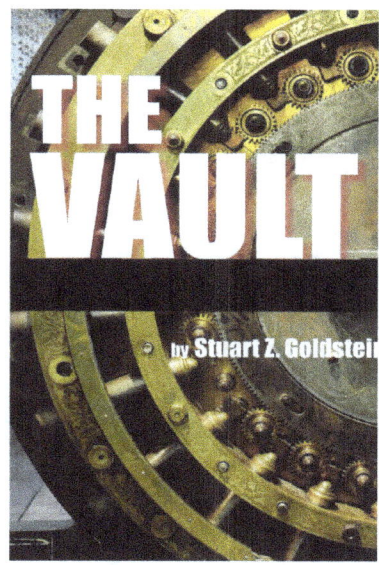

THE VAULT
Stuart Z. Goldstein

Reviewer: Jeyran Main

Stuart Z. Goldstein's The Vault is a riveting addition to the heist thriller genre. It combines high-stakes action with potent social commentary. Set in the grim underbelly of New York City, this December 2024 release takes readers three levels below the bustling streets into a world where loyalty, betrayal, and the quest for justice collide.

Andy Russo, the long-serving steward of the world's largest securities vault, is at the heart of the narrative. For four decades, Andy has toiled under a system marked by hierarchical divides, where white employees thrive above ground while immigrants and minorities endure hardship below. Frustrated by years of mistreatment, Andy reaches a critical breaking point. His decision to orchestrate a daring inside job—to steal $100 million in bearer bonds—is as much an act of personal redemption as it is a bold challenge to an oppressive order.

Goldstein skillfully constructs an environment laden with tension. The narrative's brilliance lies in its timing: as the meticulously planned heist unfolds, Hurricane Sandy races toward the city, threatening not only to flood the vault but also to obliterate the intricate plan Andy and his team have so carefully devised. This simultaneous collision of nature's fury and human ambition amplifies the stakes exponentially. It forces the characters to confront external challenges—ruthless security and encroaching chaos—and internal conflicts born of loyalty, desperation, and the moral grayness of their rebellion.

One of the most compelling aspects of The Vault is its incisive social commentary. Goldstein doesn't shy away from illuminating the systemic inequities that affect his characters. The division between those who control the high towers above and those laboring in the depths below isn't just a backdrop —it's a driving force that renders the heist both audacious and ideologically charged. Through Andy's eyes, we witness a compelling blend of personal vendetta and a broader, collective yearning for justice. The team's attempt to outsmart a system rigged to keep them down resonates as both a thrilling caper and a thoughtful exploration of class, race, and survival.

In a genre crowded with adrenaline and clever twists, The Vault stands out for its emotional depth and moral dilemmas. Goldstein's narrative is a masterclass in pacing and tension, drawing readers into a labyrinth of surprises where nothing is as it seems. With a mix of suspense, social critique, and heart-pounding action, this novel promises an electrifying journey that challenges perceptions and keeps the adrenaline pumping to its unforgettable conclusion.

Overall, The Vault is an enthralling ride—an audacious heist thriller that resonates with issues of social justice and the human condition. It's a must-read for anyone seeking a thoughtful yet pulse-pounding escape into a world where the fight for dignity is as relentless as a raging storm.

TO BE A FAE
Tricia Copeland

Reviewer: Jeyran Main

To Be a Fae by Tricia Copeland is an enchanting and intricate fantasy that invites readers into a richly imagined world where fae traditions blend with contemporary conflicts and political intrigue. The narrative centers on Queen Titania and her court as they navigate complex internal disputes and external pressures threatening to upend the delicate balance of their ethereal realm. Copeland's world-building is immersive and expansive, drawing on myth, cultural heritage, and original lore to create a vivid tapestry of fae society that feels deeply authentic.

At the novel's heart is a tapestry of interpersonal drama combined with high-stakes governance. The story opens with a charged scene in the throne room, where Titania confronts a mob of disgruntled subjects and unruly judges. Through sharp dialogue and dynamic interactions, Copeland exposes the underlying tensions among her characters, from the idealistic hope of reform to the bitter realities of power struggles and betrayal. The narrative unfolds through engaging conversations, court debates, and personal confrontations that reveal the fae's grandeur and vulnerabilities.

One of the most compelling aspects of To Be a Fae is Copeland's skillful integration of language and culture. The author employs a unique blend of modern vernacular interwoven with archaic and culturally specific terms, such as those from the Mutsun and Haudenosaunee traditions. This inventive use of language adds depth to the setting and highlights the enduring influence of ancestral customs on contemporary fae society. The reader is treated to vivid depictions of magical rites, traditional celebrations, and everyday governance that underscore the rich tapestry of fae identity.

Despite its many strengths, the novel occasionally suffers from pacing issues. Some scenes, particularly those heavy with detailed dialogue and lengthy exposition, can feel overly drawn out. However, these moments are balanced by energetic sequences of physical action and moments of levity, such as a thrilling swimming contest, that remind readers of the dynamic nature of Copeland's world.

Overall, To Be a Fae is a thought-provoking exploration of duty, heritage, and the struggle to maintain cultural identity in a rapidly changing realm. With its imaginative plot, well-crafted characters, and lush descriptions, Tricia Copeland has delivered a compelling fantasy that will resonate with readers seeking escapism and a deeper reflection on the costs and beauty of leadership in a magical world.

ETERNITY'S MIRROR
Zachary Hagen

Reviewer: Jeyran Main

Zachary Hagen's Eternity's Mirror is an ambitious and richly layered fantasy novel that plunges readers into a world where ancient magic, political intrigue, and mythical beings intertwine to create an extraordinary epic. Published in 2022, this novel invites us into a universe where relics of forgotten lore—like the Mirror of Eternity—serve as gateways to hidden realms and profound truths about power and destiny.

From the very first pages, Hagen demonstrates a masterful command of world-building. His narrative is meticulously detailed, transporting readers to diverse settings—from enchanted water sources that promise untold powers to majestic castles forged from shiny black stone, where every surface whispers secrets of bygone eras. The prose is evocative and vivid, inviting us into timeless and urgent moments. Hagen's characters, such as Elior, Nyx, and Opal, are rendered with complexity and emotion. Their dialogues and inner monologues reveal a tapestry of personal dreams and burdens, as they navigate quests that challenge their physical limits and their world's moral and ethical boundaries.

Political machinations and shifting allegiances add another layer of sophistication to the story. Ambitious rulers, treacherous betrayals, and the looming threat of a united global power, enforced by relentless djinn manipulation, drive the narrative forward. Scenes of high-stakes diplomatic meetings and covert operations are balanced by quieter, introspective moments where characters grapple with loss and the weight of destiny. The interplay between personal desire and the greater good is explored throughout, making the plot's stakes intimate and monumental.

Hagen's imaginative use of magic—from the transformative properties of enchanted water to the mysterious power of ancient artifacts—provides the perfect counterpoint to the political drama unfolding on a grand scale. The Mirror symbolizes duality, reflecting the physical world and the hidden depths of each character's soul. As the protagonists embark on a quest to unlock its secrets, they are forced to confront harsh truths about ambition, loyalty, and the sacrifices necessary to reclaim lost heritage.

Eternity's Mirror is a captivating blend of high fantasy and intricate intrigue that promises to enthrall readers who crave adventure and substance. With its compelling characters, immersive settings, and thought-provoking themes, Hagen's novel is an unforgettable journey into a realm where magic and destiny collide.